THE FEEL GOOD FACTORY ON

beating the blues

THE FEEL GOOD FACTORY ON

beating the blues

life-healing, mind-mending, soul-soothing ideas to heal a troubled mind

The Feel Good Factory led by Elisabeth Wilson

MANUFACTURED BY
THE FEEL GOOD FACTORY

This edition published in India in 2012 by

Research Press
302A, ABW Tower
MG Road
Gurgaon - 122002
India

Telephone: +91 124 4040017
Email: marketing@researchpress.co.in
Website: www.researchpress.co.in

ISBN: 9788173142550

First published in the UK by
Infinite Ideas Limited, UK

The author and publisher would like to thank Tania Ahsan, Sabina Dosani, Jackee Holder, Lynn Huggins-Cooper and Elisabeth Wilson for their contributions to this book.

Designed by D.R. Ink
Typeset by Nicki Averill

Printed by Gopsons Papers Ltd., Noida

Contents

Introduction

Is your brain full of toxins? Not physical toxins but negative thoughts, stress, unhelpful attitudes, 'I can't do that so why even try…?' – that sort of thing?

It's one thing clearing your kitchen drawer of clutter (although that can help soothe your mind). It's far harder to edit your thoughts and attitudes, and free your mind from everyday stress.

Identifying the areas of greatest anxiety in life, and the beliefs that hold you back, is an important step to ensuring your mind is calmer. Moving on in life involves prioritising what's important, what isn't, learning to know the difference – and changing your mindset so you can stop beating yourself up about everything. The next stage is taking practical steps to feel better fast. The first section of the book has plenty of strategies for just that.

If you want to feel better mentally, another sure-fire route is to feel better physically. One of the fastest routes to a healthy mind is a healthy body. In the second section there are plenty of easy ideas for nurturing and caring for your body.

In the third section, we explore ways of making every day more magical. It's so easy when life isn't going well to forget how great life can be. The third section reminds you of it.

And finally we get to the clearing-your-kitchen-drawer section, the fourth section, packed full of challenging but infinitely useful ideas for bringing clarity and focus to your life.

Different approaches will work best at different times. But adopt any one of these ideas today and you will be on the road to leaving troubles behind.

One

SOS strategies to soothe your mind

Lost your equilibrium? Does it seem impossible that you'll ever feel cool, calm and collected again? Here are emergency strategies that you can put into place immediately which will help you feel better fast.

Quiz part 1: What's bothering you?

Think about *your* personal anxieties – is it how to pay the mortgage each month, wondering what people are thinking of you, or letting everyday challenges overwhelm you?

Use our quiz to pinpoint your personal potential trouble spots and put a few simple solutions into practice. You'll find lots of stress-busting ideas in the rest of this section of the book.

Read the following statements, below.

On a scale of 0–5, rate how true each statement is for you, 0 being not at all, 3 sometimes; 5 always.

Then add up your points at the end.

1. I feel obliged to spend hours trying to make everything in my life perfect – work, the way I look, my home, the way I bring up my children – everything.
2. I dread something unexpected happening – in the office or at home. I have so many balls in the air that if my well-executed plans go awry, everything will fall apart – including me.
3. I'm surrounded by so many happy, successful and organised people. I feel a bit of a failure by comparison.
4. I worry about everyone else in my life first – I know I put others first and myself second.
5. I'm not great at relaxing – stress relief for me is a Jack Daniels and packet of filterless.

How did you score?

0–9. Sounds like you've struck the perfect balance between careful planning and realistic expectations – the recipe for the perfect enjoyable life.

10–15. While some aspects of life hold no fear for you, others are clearly a burden. Don't be pressurised – reach compromises and make sure you enjoy yourself too!

16–25. The pressure to throw yourself into all aspects of life can feel too much sometimes – wow, you need a chill pill. Ask yourself if you're enjoying the journey, or worrying too much about how you're getting there.

Quiz part 2: Stressed to breaking point?

Is your mind muddle affecting your lifestyle habits? When stress and anxiety overwhelm you, it's easy to find shortcuts and crutches – unhealthy ones at that – to help you handle it. Consider the following questions, and answer yes (score 2), sometimes (score 1) or no (score 0) to each:

1. Do you often neglect your diet?
2. Do you have unrealistic goals?
3. Do you bottle everything up?
4. Do you avoid exercise – i.e. are you 'too busy'?
5. Are you often short on sleep?
6. Do you forget to take time out each day to relax?
7. Do you worry a great deal about the past?
8. Do you feel overwhelmed by everything you have to do?
9. Do you get easily irritated by people/situations?

10. Do you often have a sense of humour failure in trying circumstances?
11. Are you a bit of a procrastinator?
12. Do you tend to lose your temper easily?
13. Are you a smoker?
14. Do you drink to relax?
15. Do you feel disorganised and out of control?
16. Do there seem to be too few hours in the day in which to get everything done?
17. Do you regularly eat fast food/skip meals?
18. Do you feel unsupported by those around you?
19. Do you ignore your feelings of stress?
20. Do you find it hard to delegate to others – at home or at work?

How did you score?

Under 14. You may experience stress but on the whole you do handle it fairly well. However, pinpoint what areas are still a problem by looking at the questions to which you answered 'yes'.

15–20. You are on the verge of being overwhelmed by stress. Take action now.

21 or over. You may be going through a particularly difficult time – or more worryingly, this is your normal state. In which case, start taking action today to reduce your stress levels.

Start by writing down how you react to stressful situations. Ask yourself what situations/people you find most stressful. Then read on to arm yourself with some good stress-busting, mind-clearing ideas.

Write it down, make it better

Ready for some therapy that's free, easily accessible and works?

Pausing to record things brings peace and serenity into troubled hearts and lives. Through keeping a diary you'll discover what really matters: what grieves you and, most importantly, what brings you joy.

Research shows that keeping a daily diary of important events, thoughts, observations, fears, disappointments, hopes, memories and distress can reduce anxiety, assuage sorrows and help you defeat depression.

Aimless ranting? Far from it. As well as putting problems on paper, keeping a diary can help you find answers for stuck or recurring problems. A diary is much more than a friend to confide in. Used effectively, diaries are supporters and collaborators in life, which is why so many people think of them as their best friend. After a few weeks you'll start to notice patterns. Some times of the week or parts of your life make you happy and they'll stick out.

Put this book down, grab a pen and paper, or sit at your computer and spend twenty minutes pouring your heart

Diaries are supporters and collaborators in life

out. This may make your worries seem more real, and that's not a good thing, but at least you know what you're really afraid of. More likely, you'll discover that your problems don't seem quite so bad when they're down on paper. Over months, your diary will be a great mood barometer, and you'll be able to use it to track your recovery and predict what you need to do to get through future tough times.

Writing creates a bit of distance that helps you be much more objective about experiences and how they make you think and feel. The great thing about putting your thoughts on paper is that you can really be yourself. We all censor ourselves when talking to friends or other helpers, but when it's just you and your journal, you can really let rip.

You may be convinced but know from past experience that you never keep to diary writing. Here are some ideas to give you structure.

- Try to write at the same time of day, as this gets momentum going and wards off inertia in other areas of your life too. You know how your moods vary during the day, so you're well placed to decide when to write. Some people like to create a soothing writing corner, with scented candles.

- Why not opt for a loose-leaf binder? You can add pages or cuttings and turn it into a valuable coping resource and this can be seen as both creative and practical. Alternatively going for the luxe factor and splashing out makes writing a more sensual experience. Invest in a beautiful journal and enjoy filling those thick vellum pages with gorgeous coloured inks.

- Follow the RED method of journal writing. When you're upset, Rant – pour it all out just as it comes to you. Finished? Now read it over and Evaluate what you've written. Try to bring some objectivity. Look for clues as to what is really upsetting you. Spot patterns of negative thinking – are you being a victim? Are you defensive? Finally Decide on a pattern of action. What three actions would make you feel better or bring relief? If there is nothing you can do, OK, make the decision to put it behind you and indulge in one of the distracting ideas in this book where you look after yourself in other ways.

- Try the 'morning pages' discipline recommended by writing guru Julia Cameron. First thing in the morning, write three pages of longhand on whatever comes into your mind. This is a fascinating exercise and helps creativity as well as your psyche. You don't need to make this a journal – write a story or poem if you feel like it.

Listen up

The right music can move you from browbeaten to bouncy in just three minutes.

Music therapy is a powerful psychological treatment that uses instrumental and vocal activities to change moods, explore feelings, promote self-expression and increase self-esteem. Ten years ago, researchers at Stanford Medical School studied thirty people with depression. The patients were randomly assigned to three groups. The first group received a weekly visit from a music therapist, the second group used music therapy techniques but didn't see a therapist, and the third group didn't have any form of musical intervention. People in the first two groups had significantly better moods and raised self-esteem and these benefits lasted. (Unless you're a metaller: scientists at the Center for the Study of Suicide, in New Jersey, found that a predilection for heavy metal was associated with suicidal preoccupations!)

- Whatever strikes a chord, listen in the dark or with your eyes closed, as your hearing will sharpen when you can't see.

- Next time you're feeling stressed, take a 'sound bath'. Put some music on your sound system, then cosy up close to the speakers. As you listen, imagine your classical harp or hiphop jazz fusion washing over you, rinsing off stresses and strains.

- Make a compilation CD or download tracks for a personalised mood-busting playlist. That way, whether you're into Motown or mountain dulcimer, you'll always have music to move you when you need a boost.

If one of the following moods describes how you're feeling, try the 'musical' prescriptions.

Sluggish. If you're having another duvet day with Enya, feel more active, alert and upbeat, by pumping up the volume with something energetic. Here are some classics:

- Irene Cara, Flashdance...What a Feeling
- Aretha Franklin, Rock Steady
- Iggy Pop, Lust for Life
- Björk, Human Behaviour (Underworld Remix)

Sad. Many pros believe that starting with music that matches your mood and then moving on to more happy, clappy sounds is the way to go. First things first; get out the tissues and play something along the lines of:

- Nick Drake, Pink Moon
- Cranberries, Disappointment

- Blur, No Distance Left to Run
- The Verve, The Drugs Don't Work

Then gradually move on to less wrist-slitting tunes and work up to full-on fun like:

- Katrina and the Waves, Walking on Sunshine
- Van Morrison, Bright Side of the Road
- Fleetwood Mac, You Make Loving Fun

Or anything else that you find impossible not to dance to or sing along to.

Scared? If you're feeling anxious, music with a slow beat will slow your breathing and racing pulse.

Don't panic, play: Brahms, Symphony Number 2.

Stuck? Upbeat instrumental music jump-starts those bits of grey matter devoted to imagination and resourcefulness. Try:

- Bach, Brandenburg Concertos
- Handel, Water Music
- Vivaldi, Four Seasons

Stressed? Slow, gentle compositions help release muscle tension and lower blood pressure. Choose music with a slow rhythm, ideally slower than your heart rate which will be about 70 beats per minute. One of these should do the trick:

- Bach, Goldberg Variations
- Pachelbel, Canon in D

Sleepy but can't sleep? Lying awake, tossing and turning? Try these songs to soothe your mind:

- Radiohead, Go To Sleep
- Air, Another Day
- The Beatles, Golden Slumbers

Slow, gentle compositions help release muscle tension and lower blood pressure

A pleasure a day …

Building enjoyment into every single day is an important life skill.

You're tired, you feel flat, fed up and life just isn't fun any more. Hardly surprising you don't feel like doing anything.

Have you stopped going out with friends, dropped out of your book club or left your bike rusting in the shed for a second consecutive Christmas? Is it such a big deal? Frankly, yes, because once you've given up enjoyable activities, you fall into a cycle that makes you feel worse and you'll end up doing even less.

How do you get out of this slump of inactivity? Remember the kind of stuff that used to make your heart soar? No matter if it was kickboxing, karaoke or knitting, it's time to do it again. When we do things we love, we forget ourselves, lose track of time and dismal thoughts take a back seat. Doing just one thing that's fun or that gives you that warm glow of achievement will make you feel better. In fact, even planning to do something you enjoy can cause a mini buzz.

Doing just one thing that's fun will make you feel better

Here's how it works:

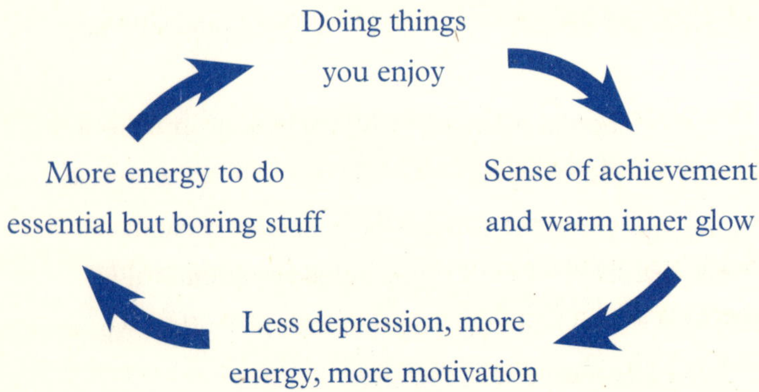

Doing what you enjoy has what pros call a 'dose–response effect'. This means that the more you do, the better you'll feel. Doing ten nice things a week is twice as good as five. But even one's better than none. It doesn't have to bust your budget or take all afternoon. Here are some ideas to lift black moods:

- Phone a friend
- Take a yoga class
- Watch a big match
- Plant a shrub
- Borrow a dog and go for a walk
- Dance to a CD
- Watch a funny film
- Have a massage

- Be a lady (or gentleman) who lunches
- Play on your kids' X-Box while they're at school

Be realistic about what you're going to do: schedule and plan and put your treats and pleasures into your diary.

Some people feel guilty about doing fun things when there's a pile of ironing to be done, mouths to feed, reports to write and deadlines looming. What they don't realise is doing things that are entertaining or exciting give us the energy to do all the less than wonderful things in life. If we deprive ourselves of pleasure, we aren't any good to anyone else. Once you've got your head round this, you'll stop feeling guilty about taking time out for yourself.

Feel good now: *Rosemary essential oil is fabulous for restoring focus. Dab it on a hanky and carry it with you or add a few drops to your conditioner so the scent travels with you all day.*

Sensual healing

When it comes to putting your troubles behind you, calming down and switching off your mind, your very best friend is your own body. Treat it well.

How we feel in our own skin – confident, happy, cherished or otherwise – impacts on other important areas of our lives such as creativity, drive, self-esteem and happiness. When we neglect our bodies, we close down to one of the easiest routes to feeling good about the world – sensual pleasure. The only way we usually indulge ourselves sensually is often through food and drink, which are fine, but limiting (and carry problems of their own if overemphasised as we'll see very shortly).

But if we open ourselves up to other ways of making ourselves feel good we discover one of the great antidotes to stress. So get in touch with your sensual self asap. Not convinced? Try the questionnaire below – remember, don't cheat: we're not measuring what you used to do, or did once when you were 19. We're talking about practices you are indulging in right now, at this point in your life.

Tick any of the following that you have done in the last two weeks.

- ☐ Massaged scented oils or lotions into your skin
- ☐ Walked into a room thinking 'I look hot' because you made an effort
- ☐ Slipped on a pair of heels to admire how they make your legs and feet look

- ☐ Bathed by candlelight
- ☐ Flirted with a stranger
- ☐ Got totally caught up listening to a song that makes you feel 10 years younger
- ☐ Made the first move in bed
- ☐ Exposed your body to a fabric that feels sensuous
- ☐ Danced in the rain
- ☐ Danced anywhere
- ☐ Watched a sunset or sunrise
- ☐ Got into bed naked
- ☐ Given yourself a thundering orgasm
- ☐ Laughed so hard you probably didn't look pretty
- ☐ Bought a beauty product that you didn't need but wanted
- ☐ Read or written erotic fiction
- ☐ Cried or laughed at a movie or a song
- ☐ Done something spontaneous because it felt really good
- ☐ Congratulated yourself on your beautiful and uplifting lingerie
- ☐ Counted the stars, preferably lying on grass
- ☐ Walked barefoot on a surface because it felt good
- ☐ Really properly hugged someone
- ☐ Really properly hugged someone who wasn't your child

How did you score?

If you ticked 5 or fewer, you are probably not feeling marvellous about yourself right now. It's hard to when you're cut off from one of your greatest sources of pleasure.

So what's the answer? Well, the questionnaire itself gives some clues. Practically everything on the list can be indulged in at any time and barely costs a penny. But working your way through the list at the rate of one a day could make a big difference to how you think about yourself.

Another way is to build an idea of yourself as a sensual person, a woman who is connected to yourself, others and the planet through your senses.

For many this is easiest through getting in touch with nature. A stroll round your garden or other green place you have ready access to in the morning or evening can transform how you view your life. Noticing the unfurling of a leaf, the spinning of a spider's web, the first flowers pushing through the earth or the way the grass smells after rain can transform a humdrum day into a thing of beauty.

Observing yourself in the same detail can be tougher but ultimately as rewarding. Embark on a month-long beautifying adventure. Make a list of all that you could do to feel better about yourself from getting your brows professionally plucked to finally finding a hair colour that makes you feel sexy and flatters your colouring. Spend a lot of time, and a little money, indulging yourself. And make part of this adventure spending a few minutes each day examining yourself in a mirror and finding only the positive about yourself. Notice how much smoother your skin gets when you moisturise it regularly; admire your still-good bone structure; marvel at how a little effort and change in eye make-up transforms your eyes. Imagine you were a dearly loved friend who was feeling bad about herself. What would you say and do for your friend to help boost her confidence? What does she need to make her feel good: a laugh, a new hair cut, a hug? What can you do to get her those things?

Treat yourself like a cherished friend, who deserves to enjoy the best things in life; indulge your sensual self as you would a little child who needs cosseting and looking after and you might begin to feel a whole lot better about life.

Spend a lot of time indulging yourself

Strategies to keep you looking great

It's not just your mind that gets twisted out of shape by stress. Worry and anxiety can make you fat. These strategies will calm you down and, as a bonus, keep you slim.

Stress causes your body to release cortisol and this stimulates the fat-storing hormone, insulin. Insulin causes your body to hold on to its fat stores.

And that's if you're eating what you always ate. The trouble is that research shows that when women especially are stressed they tend to overeat, especially carbohydrates. (It's not called comfort food for nothing.) That's because carbohydrates cause the brain to release serotonin and this is one of the feel-good hormones that raises mood. In a way, it's a form of self-medication. As is booze. Terrific at relaxing you. Fabulous for adding layers of fat to your body.

- Researchers discovered that when women ate 'off piste' whenever they wanted, they ate 120 calories a day more than those women who ate three meals and three snacks a day at set times. Decide on your meal times and stick to them. No grazing.

- Make a conscious effort to cut out salt as we feel more drawn to salty foods when we're stressed. There could

Exercise lowers stress levels and burns calories

be a physiological reason for this. Salt raises blood pressure and that in turn actually raises cortisol levels – which might have been an advantage when we only got stressed once a month but is redundant for the most part now. Wean yourself from adding salt to food and aim to eat no more than 6g of salt a day which is easily clocked up if you eat processed food.

- Caffeine raises levels of stress hormones and makes you even more stressed. Try green tea. It has about half the caffeine of coffee and a little less than black tea. And it's good for your brain and your circulation as well as your waistline. There's another advantage. A recent study found people drinking green tea lost 2–4 kg after 3 months while those who drank black tea lost only 1–3 kg. Research is ongoing to discover if the catechins in green tea trigger weight loss.

- It takes 20 minutes for our stomach to register that we've started to eat and switch off the feeling of hunger. It's certainly borne out by a small US study of women who were instructed to eat slowly, chewing carefully and swallowing their food. They were told to stop eating when their last bite didn't taste as good as the first. They lost 3.6 kg. The control group gained 1.3kg.

Our bodies know when we've had enough if we slow down long enough to listen.

- One study showed that women who make a conscious effort to relax lost an average of 4.5kg (10lb) in 18 months without consciously dieting. The truth is you need actively to relax in order to switch off the stress hormones which could be contributing to weight gain.

The best possible antidote to stress and weight gain is to exercise as it lowers stress levels and burns calories. Buy a pedometer from a sports shop and measure how many steps you take in an average day (most people average around 4,000). Gradually do more each day until you're up to 10,000.

Feel good now: *Maximise the restorative power of a bath at the end of the day by adding one or two drops of blue or green food colouring to your bath water along with your favourite bubble bath. Blue and green work powerfully on your brain to relax and calm you. But don't overdo it!*

Great rates

Getting into the habit of rating your everyday activities in a small notebook can really help you gravitate towards happiness. Rate each one for the amount of enjoyment you think you'll get from it and how much you actually get after you've achieved an activity, on a scale of 1 to 10, where 10 is the highest. The purpose is that it helps you pinpoint what you actually get most pleasure out of in life rather than what you think you get pleasure from, and conversely, it helps you recognise what may need to be dumped. It teaches you to focus on who and what really makes you happy.

Here's how it might look.

Time	*Task*	*Enjoyment perceived*	*Enjoyment actual*
8 a.m.	*Get out of bed*	*2*	*7*
9 a.m.	*Make and eat breakfast*	*4*	*6*
10 a.m.	*Listen to radio*	*6*	*5*
11 a.m.	*Go out for walk*	*4*	*7*
12 noon	*Read newspaper*	*6*	*8*
1 p.m.	*Make and eat lunch*	*4*	*5*

2 p.m. Ironing	*5*	*7*
3 p.m. Buy meal for later	*7*	*6*
4 p.m. Listen to music	*8*	*5*
5 p.m. Put away ironing	*3*	*5*
6 p.m. Candlelit bath	*8*	*7*
7 p.m. Eat ready meal	*8*	*2*
8 p.m. Phone John	*7*	*7*
9 p.m. Check emails	*6*	*8*
10 p.m. Get ready for bed	*5*	*8*
11 p.m. Read in bed	*7*	*6*

Note that some activities gave so little pleasure that it might be worthwhile making a different decision next time (cooking a meal from scratch or heating up beans on toast which might be better nutritionally than the ready meal that gave so little pleasure). Some that weren't expected to help, did (putting away the ironing may be giving a sense of achievement and control). Play with this and you may get some surprises.

Diversion ahead

Going over and over difficulties is guaranteed to make you feel even worse. Discover how to stop anxiety, fear and melancholy before they take hold.

'A man's life is what his thoughts make of it.' So said Roman emperor Marcus Aurelius, who worked hard his whole life to accept both good and bad news with equanimity. Even Roman emperors didn't get it all their own way and he knew he'd have his problems to face, too. When those problems came, refusing to get too upset about them was the quickest way through in his opinion. But how?

We spend ages mulling over problems and worries. Before you have a moment's peace to try to tackle 'em, you're weighed down and distressed. Sound familiar? Diverting your mind from them, by using distraction techniques, helps you cut down time spent brooding and also lifts your mood. Diverting your mind from pessimistic ponderings gives you back the reins when emotions are running riot. And as you're in this for the long haul, you'll have more energy to take a positive look at problems and sort them out. You'll be able to replace those thoughts with positive or at least constructive ones. Next time you notice your thoughts spinning faster than a gyroscope, try out one of these five diversions:

Using distraction techniques lifts your mood

Scramble in the attic and dig out your Rubik's cube

Next time ruminations start, put all your mental energy into getting at least one side of the same colour. Crosswords and puzzles fulfil the same function

Alphabet zoo (T is for Tarantula)

Go through the alphabet sequentially, naming an animal for each letter. If it's too easy, restrict yourself to a category like wild animals or exotic pets.

Objects of desire

Focus on an object of desire. You can choose something you own, or something you don't have, but lust after. Imagine your object, describe it to yourself in as much detail as you can. If you find this difficult, you might find these questions useful:

- What is it for?
- Where is it?
- What is it made of?
- What does it feel like?
- What colour is it?
- Does it smell of anything?
- How tall is it?
- How much does it weigh?

Space sense

Using each sense in turn, describe the space you are in.

What do the other people look like?
What might they do for a living?
What else can I see around me?
What can I hear?
What are my hands resting on?
What does that feel like?
Can I feel my clothes on my body?
What are the textures like?
What can I smell?
Can I taste anything?

You can adapt these questions to any setting.

Think of a number

While you're at it, think of two: a big number and a small one. Take the small number away from the bigger one. Now take the smaller number away from your answer. Keep going as far as you can, even when you're into negatives.

Get in touch with your creativity

Some profoundly clever people think one of the reasons so many of us are unhappy is because we're taught to suppress our creativity.

The good news is that it is never too late to reclaim it.

Art seems to serve a primal urge in many people. Researchers found that a ten-week course of art therapy significantly reduced symptoms of depression in people with an insoluble problem, Alzheimer's disease. Art gave them a way of expressing things that were beyond words or even comprehension.

You don't need to be Picasso to make the most of art therapy. The knack is to think of art therapy with a small a and capital T. The onus is on healing rather than award-winning pictures or objects. Even geniuses don't get it right first time. Picasso's masterpiece Guernica was only created after numerous different attempts at finding the right approach. Instead of waiting for the perfect idea to emerge, force yourself to have lots of imperfect ones.

Other studies have shown that undertaking art projects increases self-esteem, decreases anxiety, improves mood and helps us cope better with stress.

Think more creatively.

If you already know what creative pursuit you'd like to embrace, terrific. If not, you can still start thinking more creatively. Try these:

Each morning, undertake 'the breakfast brainstorm' (or you could slot this in during your morning commute – the point is to spend five minutes a day doing this routinely). Think of what you most desire today and frame it as a question: 'How do I find a job I love?', 'How do I find the cash to go to a health spa?', 'How do I find a creative activity that I'll enjoy?' Start scribbling ideas, the more off-the-wall the better because that will 'free' your mind to think in different ways. Keep going until at least one feasible idea evolves. Besides being a solution, one bonus to doing this regularly is that it opens your mind up to myriad possibilities and will help you think more creatively about every decision and problem you encounter.

Think more creatively about every decision and problem you encounter

Another way of seeking new stimuli is to encourage the non-dominant part of your brain. We tend to be left (logical) brain-dominated (which is why more of us are right-handed as the left-hand brain controls the right-hand side of the body). Brain studies show that creative people use the right-hand (creative) part of their brain more than the rest of us. Encouraging the connection between the two hemispheres boosts right-brain thinking.

So use your non-dominant hand to complete tasks such as brushing your teeth or loading the washing machine – it builds those right–left brain connections. By making your brain undertake the familiar in an unfamiliar way, you are lowering your latent inhibition levels.

Actively look for ways of allowing your creative juices to flow. Just about anything can be a creative act if you reframe it in those terms. From working to make your meals look and taste more delicious; to finally redecorating the spare room; to planting some pretty pots for your windowsill; to wearing clothes that make you feel wonderful and express who you truly see yourself as being, putting creativity at the centre of your life will reap huge rewards in terms of making you feel good.

Coco Chanel's feel-good secrets

The woman who invented modern fashion, and all-round icon, did not have an easy life. Here's what life taught her.

'How many cares one loses when one decides not to be something but to be someone.'

'I don't understand how a woman can leave the house without fixing herself up a little – if only out of politeness. And then, you never know, maybe that's the day she has a date with destiny. And it's best to be as pretty as possible for destiny.'

'There is no time for cut-and-dried monotony. There is time for work. And time for love. That leaves no other time.'

'Plain women know more about men than beautiful women do.'

Two

Love your body, heal your mind

Looking after your health, by building stress-relieving habits into your routine is probably the most constructive thing you can do to make yourself feel better.

Quiz:
How healthy is your attitude to exercise?

If you want to lift your mood, think more clearly and be more creative; exercising is about the most productive thing you can do. And of course, ensuring you take regular exercise also boosts your energy levels – there's no better instant revitaliser – and that makes you feel much better about life, too.

1. How often do you take exercise?

(a) Constantly – I'm a three-times-a-week or more kind of person.

(b) Rarely – unless you include nightclubbing, playing footie or rounders in the park, the odd salsa class – that's once a week or so.

(c) I'm not a natural exerciser – I'm more of a philosopher, really.

2. What do you think of Pilates?

(a) It's a fantastic discipline for the abs and girdle muscles generally. It helps my posture, relieves aches and pains and makes my limbs feel much longer.

(b) I've tried it once, but I prefer something a bit more up-tempo.

(c) I think they do a really important job, but I bet flying isn't really as glamorous as it seems.

3. Which most appeals to you as a discipline?

(a) Kettle bell training. It's reduced my body fat dramatically and talk about abs of steel.

(b) I prefer music-based dance classes – I prefer to follow an instructor and shake my stuff.

(c) Mmm, that Kettle Chip training sounds right up my boulevard.

4. How do you define your relationship with exercise?

(a) I need it – it's part of my life and without it I'd feel lacking in vitality and lethargic.

(b) I'm pretty balanced about most things – sometimes I'm not in the mood for exercise, but I'm always pleased once I start the class.

(c) We're seldom on speaking terms.

5. If you over-indulge how do you react?
(a) I wouldn't do anything too strenuous after a hangover – but I'd probably take a brisk walk or hike, swim twenty lengths – cycle a few miles, that sort of thing.
(b) Feel a bit guilty, but I compensate by moving a bit more during the week.
(c) Full up, hungover perhaps – but no more inclined to show my spare tyre to the weirdy gym fraternity.

How did you score?

Mostly As:

Are you for real? Congratulations, you're one of the lucky ones – a born athlete and not short of get and up and go. Sounds like you're clearly in love with exercise. But it obviously isn't doing what it used to do in terms of making you feel good. Could it be that it's become another chore? Put some fun back into your exercise routine. Put some fun back into your life in general. It might be time to loosen up rather than up your activity.

Mostly Bs:

You're probably someone who enjoys the social aspect of exercise, but may have signed up to a regular workout, so probably aren't pushing your body enough to get real benefits. Try:

- Making sure you exercise three times a week for about 30 minutes each time – break it up into ten minute slots if it's easier.
- Try a new class at the gym – experimenting with new disciplines may work parts of the body you often overlook.
- Write a list of how good you feel after you have taken some exercise – more exercise equals more feel-good rewards.
- Sign up for a session with a personal trainer – or split the cost with a friend. He or she may help set new goals that can keep you motivated.

Mostly Cs:

Sounds like your relationship with exercise could be described as 'disordered'. Try:

- Teaming up with a friend to go walking or cycling – once a week at first and build up.
- Get yourself some groovy workout gear – studies on teenage girls show that looking good can help you stay committed to an exercise regime.

- Write a list of the disciplines that do interest you – then do a bit of research, or go wild and try a class.
- Go for a health check – it's a sure-fire way to get you off that bar stool and into your trainers.
- Read the ideas here to get you started. The first one in this section will start you off and research shows that any form of self-care helps motivate you to exercise.

Exercising 101

So now you're convinced that you should exercise for the sake of your mind as well as your body, where do you start?

This exercise programme works equally well for first-time exercisers or those returning to regular exercise. If it's too easy for you, move it up a gear, or jump some steps. But beware. Research has shown that there are two reasons that exercise programmes fail:

- We don't see the results we want (that's dealt with below): or
- We set our expectations too high.

It's far better to do a little and stick to it until you have the exercise habit than go nuts, join a gym, write an ambitious exercise programme and then give up completely after a couple of weeks of failure to keep to it.

Decide on your goal

If you've never exercised before, or have lapsed, please start with a modest goal. If it's ten minutes of activity a day – that's brilliant, as long as you're confident that you'll do it. Aim to visit your local pool once a week, then three times a week. Aim to swim once a week and walk round the park once a week. Aim to do a yoga class on a Saturday morning.

Make your plan

You need a schedule where every week you are aiming to do a little more, a little more frequently until you are exercising for around three to four hours a week – enough to get you out of breath for most of the time. This could take a year, but don't think about that now. Stick your monthly schedule on the fridge. At first your goal should be just to stick to your weekly plan. Once you've got the hang of it, you can make your goal bigger, such as: run round the park, undertake your local fun run, cycle to the next town then cycle back.

Aim for cardiovascular exercise to begin with

If you are very exhausted, very unfit, have been ill or are very overweight, all you might be able to manage is walking up the stairs. Fine. Make that your goal: to walk up stairs three times a week, then five times a week, and so on from there. Aim for cardiovascular exercise to begin with, that gets your heart beating, because that's the type that will give you energy fastest.

Here is the easiest programme you can adapt to your favourite exercise:

Week 1: Walk slowly for five minutes, walk briskly for five minutes, walk slowly for five minutes. Aim to do that for three days a week.

Week 2: Aim to do the same five times a week.

Week 3: Walk slowly for ten minutes, walk briskly for ten minutes, walk slowly for ten minutes. Aim for four times a week.

Week 4: Walk slowly for five minutes, walk briskly for twenty minutes, walk slowly for five minutes. Aim for five times a week.

From this, start increasing the time you walk briskly and reduce the time you take it easy. Remember the acronym FIT: frequency, intensity, time per session. First work on frequency – aim to do some form of exercise five or six times a week. Then work on 'T' – the time you spend at it each time you do it. Then move on to the intensity – use hills to make you work harder, or go faster, or try a more difficult stroke if you're swimming.

If you are still struggling, think of hooking up with a buddy. Research proves that a friend will encourage and support you, and make it more likely that you will keep to your programme.

Eat yourself happy

What you eat can have a dramatic effect on your mood.

The most important fact to remember when you are talking about lifting mood through diet, is that eating regularly is an absolute must. Without regular food intake – no more than three hours without eating – our blood sugar levels plummet and we find it hard to concentrate. Just like little children, we get cranky and cross – we are just better at hiding it. And in some cases not that good at hiding it at all.

The basics of a healthy diet – wholegrain foods, lots of fruit and vegetables, some high-quality protein on a daily basis – are what's needed to feel your best, but there are some key nutrients that are worth boosting if you are particularly frazzled or low. Eating small, regular meals is often the answer to transforming energy levels both physically and mentally.

Fish oils

Depression is about ten times commoner in Europe and North America than in Taiwan. It's also rarer in Hong Kong and Japan where they eat a lot of fish. Researchers

Eating regularly is an absolute must

have found that the omega-3 oils found in fish – which is a dietary staple in the East – helps severely depressed, even suicidal patients. Fish and seafood provide the complex omega-3 most important to the brain.

Don't eat fish? You'll need to count on your body converting a simpler fat called alpha-linolenic acid (ALA), into omega-3. The easiest way to include ALA in your diet is by munching nuts and seeds. Walnuts, brazil nuts and flaxseed are your best bet. And go organic. Organic milk contains 70% more omega-3 than standard milk.

Iron

Many women in the UK are chronically short of iron without realising it. If you're low in iron, you'll be tired and less likely to be up for any mood-boosting exercise. Rev up your iron stores by putting some red meat on the table at least twice a week. Roast beef, venison and calfs liver are all good sources. If you don't eat meat, consider supplements.

Tryptophan

Cravings could be a sign of low levels of the neurotransmitter, serotonin. To increase serotonin levels, eat protein-containing foods that are rich in the amino acid tryptophan such as milk, turkey, chicken sandwiches, dates and hazelnuts.

Watch out for:

Caffeine and alcohol. Caffeine overconsumption has made depression worse in some studies; it can also make you jittery and panicky without you realising it (you just keep blaming it on a bad day). Alcohol helps you relax but it acts to depress the central nervous system and that adversely affects mood and also makes it difficult to make decisions.

Out of your head

Here's a way of handling stress that could improve just about every other aspect of your life too.

Mindfulness is a way of relaxing your mind and becoming aware of what's actually happening in the present. It comes out of the work of Jon Kabat-Zinn, a scientist who runs stress-reduction programmes to help seriously ill people. He wanted to find a way to teach patients how to kick-start their own healing powers. Like meditation, mindfulness gives control by helping you to listen to your body.

Lie down (although you can do this sitting if it is more convenient). It helps at first to close your eyes. Become aware of your breathing. Don't force deep breaths but 'see' in your mind your breath entering through your nostrils and flooding your lungs. Listen to the sounds of your breath. Concentrate on nothing else. When your mind wanders, let these thoughts float away, imagining them as little white clouds, and then return to the breath.

That's it.

It's recommended you be mindful for 45 minutes a day for best results. But if you can manage just 5 minutes you will find it helps immensely in bringing stress levels down. It keeps you calm even when things get hairy and is especially good for helping you maintain your sense of humour. It does indeed aid healing and lower blood pressure.

It isn't as easy as it sounds. Stopping and listening and just being allows you to access great joy and happiness, but it also makes it hard to ignore feelings of grief and anger and disappointment that surface when you stop whirling around in a frantic rush. Kabat-Zinn says that mindfulness helps his patients decide what they really want from life and after it becomes second nature to become still and focused he recommends that you ask yourself questions during your sessions such as 'what do I truly love?' and 'where am I going?'.

The point is to become aware of the here and now. It is quite shocking how much time we spend in the past or fantasising about the future. We forget that the present is a great place to be – because in the present we are nearly always absolutely OK with the potential to be having a calm and productive day.

Mindfulness gives control by helping you to listen to your body

Learn to bounce

Each of us is born with a happiness set point that is genetically influenced, but crucially, not fixed. We learn from others that life is fixed, that we can't change, that we're not in control. But that's wrong. The thing to remember is this: your brain chemistry is not fixed.

No matter how unhappy you are right now, you can change it positively.

You can learn to bounce back from problems, a skill some are lucky enough to be born with but one that all of us can learn.

How? When bad stuff happens, ask yourself what's known as coping questions which challenge inflexible thinking. What would be useful for me to do right now? What is the reality, and what is merely my fantasy about this situation? Can I salvage anything from this? What could I learn from it if I saw it as an opportunity? What could I do to turn this around?

Bad stuff happens to good people all the time. Whether you let it pull you down depends on your expectations. Look at the number of people who have lost fortunes, businesses, everything – and then very quickly become wealthy and successful again. Their expectation was that they would. If your expectation is that you'll learn and prosper through difficult times, you will, too.

Ready for a detox?

Take some of the strain off your body and you'll feel lighter in your mind too.

If you drink a lot of alcohol, simply eliminating the booze for a few days might constitute a detox diet and help you feel immediately better. If your diet is quite pure, you might have to go on a fruit fast to get the same benefits.

The point is that by putting less strain on your body's eliminating organs (the liver, kidney and guts primarily), you find you have more energy. A good side effect is that the distraction offered by preparing for and sticking to a detox diet can help take your mind off your worries.

Retreating from the world for a weekend, eliminating everything but fruit and water and spending the time relaxing and resting is all that's needed to get a bit of a boost. If that doesn't sound like you, here is a way of helping yourself to the benefits without too much strain, and still living in the real world.

Choose in the first week to eliminate coffee, chocolate and caffeine drinks and replacing them with lots of water and herbal teas. In the second week, try eliminating wheat products (cake, biscuits, pasta) and eating protein and vegetables with rye bread, brown rice, quinoa, buckwheat or millet. In the third week, try substituting dairy products for sheep and goat's milk and cheese and in the fourth drink loads of water while eliminating alcohol. That fourth week should give you a terrific sense of achievement if nothing else.

Doctors will tell you that detoxing is a waste of time, but they underestimate the mental benefits. It demands discipline and that makes you feel better about yourself. And giving your body a bit of a break from a 21st century diet certainly won't do it any harm. It could change the way you think about food forever.

Feel good now: *This yogic breathing has been shown to 'wake up' your brain. Close off your right nostril with the thumb of your right hand and breathe in through your left for the count of four. Now close off your left nostril with the index finger of your right hand and exhale for the count of four. Breathe in through your right nostril, and then out through the left, closing off your right nostril with your thumb. Repeat half a dozen times. This is great for relaxing you at any time of the day.*

Wash your way to well-being

When is a bath not a bath? When it's this restful, refreshing spa treatment that will nourish and cleanse your body and spirit – and you don't have to travel further than your own bathroom.

Try this Zen bath and you'll see why the Japanese consider having a bath to be a sacred experience.

This version of the Japanese bath works very well mid-week, on a 'school night', and if you make time for it once a week, you'll soon feel the benefits all through the week. It works better than a simple candle-lit bath to relax you because you have to put a (minimal) amount of effort in and that makes you feel you're taking back control. The Japanese bath has cumulative effects – the more often you do it, the more powerfully it works. There is a set pattern to it and the predictability is soothing in itself.

You will need: a balancing essential oil such as lavender or geranium or frankincense, an aromatherapy burner, a quiet place to sit, a clean bathroom (free of clutter), some soft towels (preferably warmed), a loofah or a body brush or sisal glove, a small bowl, comfortable clothes, a teapot, cup, strainer, loose-leaf tea, a candle, a blanket, and a minimum of one hour. Invest in some special props that you keep purely for this restoration bath. The sense of 'specialness' helps turn a bath into an event and with time you will be able to trigger relaxation with just part of the ritual. A cup of tea, a bath with the balancing oil or body brushing will in themselves be almost as good as the whole ritual.

The more often you do it, the more powerfully it works

First, light the burner in the bathroom, lock the door and sit there quietly breathing in the fragrance, letting your mind quieten and be still. Lay your hands on your stomach, breathe in deeply and feel your stomach move out. Breathe out and feel your stomach contracting. Let go of all other thoughts. Now, and for the rest of this hour, keep your focus on what you can see, feel, hear and smell. Anxious thoughts will intrude, of course. When they do, imagine them drifting off in the fragrance rising from the burner.

When you're relaxed, undress and gently draw a brush or loofah over your body, working always towards the heart. Then step into the shower – it works best if it is at a slightly cooler temperature than usual. Lather up and get really clean. Concentrate on the noise of the shower. Let anxious thoughts disappear down the plughole with the soapy water.

Clean? Now step out of the shower and run yourself a hot bath. Add a few drops of your balancing oil to the rushing water. Sink into the bath. When intrusive, worrying thoughts interrupt, let them gently float away in the steam. When you're good and chilled out, use the small bowl to ladle water all over your body. The idea is not to get clean but to focus your mind on pouring the water as gracefully as possible. Study the pattern of the falling water. Let yourself enter a sort of trance state, soothed by the repetitive actions. When thoughts of the outside world intrude, imagine them moving from your mind to being plastered on your body and then visualise them being swept away by the falling water.

When your mind is calm and you feel centred, emerge, wrap yourself in warm towels, dry off and dress in warm, comfortable clothing.

Hold this 'mindful' state. Go to a peaceful corner of your home and light a candle. (If you can do this whole ritual by candlelight, it will be even more restful.) Then make some tea, concentrating fully on every step. Watch the kettle boil, relax and breathe deeply and keep your mind as restful as possible. Concentrate on the candlelight if it helps. Make your movements as graceful and economical as possible. Green tea gives the authentic 'Eastern' feeling. Herbal is good. But any tea will do. Finally, retire to your quiet place, cosy up with a blanket, sip your tea, inhale the fragrance, focus on the candle flame, keep your attention on it. Concentrate on the taste of the tea. Imagine anxious thoughts drifting away in the fragrant steam rising from your cup.

Sleep deep

Some simple strategies to help you make the most of your time in bed.

The most reliable predictor of depression is insomnia. Sleeping less than six hours a night is linked to increased obesity and sleeping less than seven hours night linked to increased mortality.

If you have trouble sleeping, it's worth reiterating that insomnia is like losing weight. It's not enough to know what to do, you have to act on it. 'Chronic' insomniacs often stay up half the night drinking tea or alcohol, smoking and watching movies. And they go to bed and listen to the radio and read until finally about 4 a.m., they doze off . If you don't sleep well here are some key strategies.

- Don't drink caffeine for at least six hours before bed.
- Eschew alcohol and cigarettes for at least four hours before bedtime.
- Don't look at any sort of screen for three hours before bedtime.
- Get outside every day and do some exercise.

Keep up all of the above for three weeks.

If this doesn't work the best advice is to think of yourself as a little child. Infants are not born with the ability to soothe themselves to sleep, they need to learn the skill. They do that through routine.

Stop all chores and any form of work at least two hours before bedtime. Develop a wind-down routine that starts about an hour before bed. Gentle yoga is brilliant for this, or you could lie on the sofa and listen to quiet music. Then run a hot bath. The bath is important. To counteract the heat your body lowers its temperature. Lowered body temperature triggers sleep. For that reason your bedroom and bed should verge on the cool. Cosy down in bed and read a book that isn't too thrilling and requires a little effort: Shakespeare, Jane Austen, Dickens.

Do this every single night for a week.

If this doesn't work, get radical. You cannot sleep. You either can't get off to sleep or you wake early but you spend an inordinate amount of time tossing and turning. So don't. Just get up and do something else. See your insomnia as a gift. It's the chance to improve your life, to carve out some time for yourself. If you wake at 4 a.m. and then spend the rest of the night tossing and turning, set your alarm for 4.30 and get up instead. After a few days you might discover an optimal time when you can get up and be productive. If you can sleep for around 6 hours, and fit in a nap, you might find that it's enough. A long nap will not help you sleep but a short one of half an hour or so will not put you off your sleep at night and may prove a routine that you can stick to.

Remember also that one of the keys to a restful night's sleep is to get your brain calm rather than revved up. So you need to avoid foods that perk you up. Steer clear of foods containing the amino acid tyrosine – found in bacon and cured meat. Opt for those that contain tryptophan found in milk – a milky drink might just be the ticket before bed.

Cosy down in bed and read a book

Relax regularly

The solution to the eternal problem of finding enough time to look after yourself is to build rock-solid relaxation time into your schedule and treat your appointment to relax as seriously as you do any other.

If at all possible book a professional therapy session once a week. Failing that, once a week schedule time for a DIY session at home.

Two professional treatments that you can easily adapt for home use are flotation and reflexology.

Flotation

Floating naked in pitch darkness and utter silence for an hour at a time in heavily salted water may seem like a strange way to relax but it can be amazingly relaxing. Sensory deprivation is the closest you can get to experiencing the security and comfort of the womb. You are all alone with your thoughts and that can be a bit shocking at first. Once you get used to being up close and personal with what's in your brain without any distractions, it can inspire great creativity as well as almost mystical experiences. If you can treat yourself to a monthly float, it will do wonders for your stress levels.

A monthly float will do wonders for your stress levels

DIY version

Run a bath as deep as you can. Empty one packet of Dead Sea salts or Epsom salts (at least 500g) into your bath. Make the bathroom as dark as possible. Set an alarm clock for half an hour. Soak in the bath and sip herbal tea or water throughout to prevent dehydration. (Hot drinks increase perspiration, which is good.) Don't do this if you are pregnant, have high blood pressure or any kind of heart problem. Don't dry off after your bath, but wrap yourself in towels and go straight to bed. Be careful. You may feel light-headed. When you wake, have a warm bath or shower.

Reflexology

Ancient Egyptian tomb paintings depict scenes of pharaohs getting their feet treated. Reflexology is a very ancient treatment. It is far more sophisticated than a mere foot rub. Having your feet cradled and massaged grounds you and is instantly calming. The theory is that all nerves originate in the spine and branch out through the body but ultimately all connect with the nerves that end in the foot. Each area of the foot therefore corresponds to an area of the body.

DIY version

First relax your feet in a foot bath into which you've added some tepid water and few drops of peppermint oil.

Then gently massage your feet using your thumb to make small circling movements over the whole sole of each foot. When you find a tender spot, work on it gently – this indicates an area where you have tension. Look for the spot just under the joint of the little toe. It corresponds to the shoulders – a place where many of us carry tension.

Madonna's life rules

One person who knows how to push herself through insecurities and doubt is Madonna. How does she do it?

'Poor is the man whose pleasures depend on the permission of another.'

'When I'm hungry, I eat. When I'm thirsty, I drink. When I feel like saying something, I say it.'

'I believe that we are responsible for our own fate, we reap what we sow, we get what we give, we pull in what we put out. I know these things for sure.'

Three

Make every day extraordinary

It's not the big stuff that brings us down or stresses us out. Often it's the mundane. The drag of the 9 to 5, the relentlessness of having to keep producing three meals a day for the family, the drudgery of feeling that there must be more than this. But it doesn't have to be that way. Here we look at little ways of making your every day magical.

Quiz:

What are your work problem areas?

Since most of us spend more time at work than we do with loved ones, examining our attitudes to the 9 to 5 can give valuable clues as to why we've lost our zing. Let's take a few minutes to examine your working life. This quiz should help highlight the issues which may be holding you back.

Tick one answer in each section, imagining what would be the most likely answer you'd give if the situation applied to your life.

1. You wake up at 7.30 on a Monday morning and your first thought about work is:

(a) Oh no, I meant to wake up at 6 a.m. this morning to fine tune that presentation. I'll have to work through lunch – again. ☐

(b) Just one more glorious day on the mind-numbing treadmill of life. ☐

(c) Urgh, that project's due today and I'm only half-way through. Perhaps I can say the computer crashed or the dog ate it. ☐

(d) If that Mr Snodgrass from logistics dares give me another lecture today about my poor presentation skills, I'll say something. I really will. ☐

2. At last, there's a chance for promotion moving into the next division. The interview involves a lot of work – and it won't be easy. Which of the following statements best sums up your attitude?

(a) I'm sure I'm the best candidate for the job, and I've some great ideas for the interview project. I'll have to come in on Sunday to prepare of course. ☐

(b) Not sure, it's a big leap. Perhaps I should consolidate here for a few months. Really perfect my skills. Show them I'm no lightweight. ☐

(c) I've every intention of applying for that job. But I really have to finish filing my paperclips, and then there's the pencil-sharpening to be done. ☐

(d) Great job, but old Snodgrass will put the spanner in the works – sod's law. ☐

3. You're highly praised for an important project well done. How do you react?

(a) Just as well I didn't go home at all last week. That office floor may not be cosy – but what's a bit of arthritis compared with such glory? ☐

(b) Great, now if I can repeat that for the next three years I'll be getting somewhere. ☐

(c) I'll be sure to add that to my CV when I get a moment next month. ☐

(d) Ha ha, Snodgrass – foiled again. ☐

4. It's your annual review. How will you approach it?

(a) Now this needs preparation. Perhaps if I cancel my trip to the Seychelles next week I can get some thoughts together. ☐

(b) I'll tell them how happy I am and how much I've learned in this, my 12th year on the desk. ☐

(c) I'm currently compiling a list of my achievements over the past year. Should be ready by the next review. ☐

(d) Be afraid Snodgrass – I'm going public... or maybe next time. ☐

How did you score?

Mostly As:

Looks like poor time management is keeping you from your just rewards. You may impress the suits – but at what cost? Start by reviewing your time management. How much can you delegate? Every day, write an achievable, realistic to-do list – factoring in how long each meeting/document/phone call will take you – erring on the side of caution. Every day take breaks. Go out of the building. This helps your brain reorganise and focus. Remember, plan, plan, plan. And go home on time. Check out sections 3 and 4 for some more ideas.

Mostly Bs:

You're stagnating. Take a long hard look at yourself. What's keeping you tied to your desk? Lack of confidence, energy, motivation? Start by taking a piece of paper and think sky blue. Where do you really want your career to go? What do you really want from your working life? Write down a few fantasy thoughts – setting up on your own, moving to another firm, making a complete career change. Then devise five steps that can take you from where you are now, to where you want to be. There are more ideas in this section and the next to help you.

Mostly Cs:

We're all guilty of procrastinating occasionally. Boy, you've made it an art form. So you want to get the prize, win that promotion, make your first million. Plan your goals. Firstly, make a list of all you've achieved – sales figures, projects done and dusted, new business deals, that triumph with the client. Keeping a record of your achievements is useful – have it at your fingertips. Get on top of work piles. Each day write a list of tasks to be done. Do the least attractive one first. The rest will seem like a breeze. See section 4 for some more ideas.

Mostly Ds:

Office politics has you by the goolies, clearly. If it's genuine bullying you need to know your rights – see your line manager or HR officer. But perhaps you need to fine tune your communication and assertiveness skills. See this section and the next for some help.

Happy homebody

Is commuting getting you down?
Do workplace politics leave you cold?
Consider working from home and leave all
that stress behind you.

Ask yourself what you like about the work you are doing now. Perhaps constant crowds are not your 'thing' and you are thinking about downshifting to the country, and moving towards self-sufficiency. But if you enjoy office banter, enjoy 'teambuilding' exercises, delight in office politics, and crave the next instalment of gossip around the water cooler, working from home may not be for you.

However, you may prefer to have more chances to order your own day. Working at home gives you the opportunity to organise your work so that if you need to go to a meeting at school, or visit a nearly empty open garden, you can. That doesn't mean homeworking is all about slacking – you still need to get the work done, but you can do it at a time that suits you and your family.

Being around for family may be your main motivator in deciding to work from home full time. Especially if you have young children they will like having mum or dad pick them up from school every day, and coming home for lunch daily.

Teenagers like having easy access to a parent, too – and not just for handouts! Being available at incidental times of the day gives you the opportunity for many more of the 'casual' chats teenagers have with you in passing – when they tell you about the stuff that really matters in their lives.

Are you lonesome…?

Working at home can be isolating. Before you decide to work at home, check that you will enjoy the peace and calm. If you feel lonely and crave company, homeworking may not be for you. If you are happy with your own company, go for it. Some jobs such as writing demand quite a high degree of concentration, so minimising distractions and working at home during the quiet of the day may help. If you want company, you can always go out – it's as simple as that.

The main disadvantage of homeworking is the likelihood of distraction. Beware the household tasks that suddenly shout at you as you gaze round the room; shoo away the cats that flop down thunderously on a keyboard, or decide to play football with your equipment; ignore dogs that noisily demand walks – but most of all, let your friends and family know that sometimes you must not be disturbed.

Beware the household tasks that suddenly shout at you

I'm not sure whether some people don't actually believe that you are working because you are at home, but the interruptions are regular. You have to decide which ones are acceptable or welcome – good friends who ring up and ask if they can call in for coffee and won't be offended by a refusal – and which you have to discourage.

Feel good now: *Set your alarm 15 minutes early – and just lie in bed.*

Loving work

What do you do if your job is dragging you down?

To find work that will energise, excite and stimulate you, you will have to do some soul searching and perhaps face some hard decisions. Use the five words often called the journalist's best friends. They are the start of any investigation – namely, when, what, why, how and where.

1. When do you lose yourself?

Think back to the last time you were so completely engrossed in what you were doing that you didn't notice time passing. Were you painting a room, listening to your friend talk, dancing at a wedding, decorating a cake? Were you driving, shopping, helping your child with homework, volunteering for a local charity? Write it down. Try to remember a few more occasions. It might help to remember what you used to love as a child. Did you love to wander about the garden examining flowers and rocks? Were you always at the swimming pool? Did you prefer to be alone, or hang out with friends? Search for your passion. Seek out your joy. Look at your list, and mull on it.

2. What do you dream about?

Another version of step 1 is to think about what you'd do if you won the lottery and didn't have to work any more. How would you choose to spend your time if you didn't have any financial restraints? Any clues there?

3. Why are you scared?

Ask why you're not fulfilling your dream. At the root of it will almost certainly be fear. That could be fear of telling your spouse you want to give up your lucrative job to become a windsurf instructor, it could be the fear that giving up a profession into which you've invested a lot of time makes you look a fool. The longer you've studied or worked at a profession the harder it is to give it up. Think of it this way: you're not giving up, you're transferring skills: you're not wiping years off your CV, you are using past skills to find a parallel career that gives you satisfaction.

4. How much value can you add?

It may take a while. In the meantime, try putting your most into the job you've got. Bringing a good attitude to work will almost certainly result in you doing well because most people simply don't. Their work is mediocre, and that makes it easy to shine if you put in some effort. Being enthusiastic will make work pass faster.

5. Where are the soulmates?

Go back to your step 1 list. While you're looking, or retraining for your dream job, include more of what makes you happy in your life. Pursuing what makes you happy means you'll meet other people who share your interests, and who knows where that will take you? Listen to your instincts. One day you will be talking to an acquaintance when you'll get an idea 'I should do that'.

Search for your passion. Seek out your joy

The energy drench

Convert your shower into a daily spa treatment that will energise and revive you.

This will do you far more good than hitting the snooze button, or an extra shot of coffee. It will take about two minutes longer than your usual shower, but it does a whole lot more than get you clean.

One minute to invigorate your skin before you get in the shower

Buy a natural-bristle skin brush – not so hard that it hurts your skin when you pass it over the back of your hand, but hard enough so that you feel it. Use this brush prior to showering. Brush over your skin, working from your feet up your legs, from your hands up your arms and over your back and torso, always working towards your heart. The theory is that this works to boost lymph flow, which means that waste products are eliminated from your body faster. There's no evidence for this. What is for sure is that brushing causes blood to flood the surface of the skin and thus increases circulation which is a powerful tonic.

30 seconds to rub away the old

Continue to stimulate your system with a body scrub using a sisal glove or a face cloth. Plain old soap will do but a cleansing scrub with a citrus scent will wake you up even more. You can make your own scrub with a handful of coarse grain salt to which you add a few drops of lemon, grapefruit or bergamot essential oil. Put some on your glove or cloth and rub your body vigorously. This action will get rid of dead skin cells, softening your skin and invigorating you at the same time.

Two minutes to drench your body

Turn on the tap and wash away your scrub with some warm water. Then change the temperature gauge to quite cool, and stay for one minute. Return to hot again for a minute or so, and then back to cool for a final minute. The shock of passing between warm and cool will also boost your circulation. The capillary walls (those of the smallest blood vessels) are strengthened and skin tone is improved.

30 seconds to carry on the good work all day

Finally 'mist' your body with oil. Make your own 'mister' by purchasing a spray pump from a chemist or recycling one that used to contain another product. For each 100ml of water, add half a teaspoon of olive or almond oil and ten drops of an energising oil. Bergamot, lemon or rosemary are all good.

A cleansing scrub scented with citrus will wake you up

Create a sanctuary

Imagine a place with no phone, no noise,
no hassle, no problems.

Peace is a state of mind, but it's a lot easier to achieve on a daily basis if you have a special place you can retire to and instantly feel relaxed. Having a place to call your own helps immeasurably with stress. Why? Because in some very profound way, having a corner where you can let your imagination run free and where you have control is deeply important to the human spirit. As a child did you have a secret place where you would hide away? Did you build 'shrines'? No? Think of the times you set up your favourite toys next to your bed, your dolls aligned looking just right on a shelf, 'special' power stones hidden in a secret place only you knew about? Children love talismans and can spend hours contemplating a feather, a flower, a broken bottle. This is how they de-stress away from their parents, in a world of their own where they choose objects that soothe them and where they decide their significance, not the grown-ups.

Creating a place where you can go that is uniquely yours, where you have chosen what you look at, what you feel, hear and smell will prove invaluable in your battle against stress. A room is ideal, a cupboard will do, a corner of a room – just one armchair will be enough.

There you are in control and you can read, rest, dream, just be. It could be a seat in your garden, a daybed in the spare room, a dressing table where you can experiment with make-up and your image, or simply a shelf or windowsill on which you grow some flowers. But it should be so attractive to you that you long to sink into your sanctuary – that way you'll want to carve out a little time for yourself as often as possible so you can be there. And that's the essence of relaxation.

Still stuck? Write down what taste, scent, sensation, sound and sight immediately relaxes you and gather them in one place so they are always at hand. Velvet slippers, satin quilts, birdsong, pink light, roses, gardenia scented candle? What sensual cues calm you down instantly? Pack them in a box you keep under your bed and make yours a portable sanctuary you can reach for whenever you need peace.

Having a place to call your own helps immeasurably with stress

Morning glory

When an animal wakes, it stretches to get rid of tension and reawaken muscles. You should do the same.

You'll feel better but you'll also be more flexible and toned and get rid of minor aches and pains.

This 10-minute yoga routine is a great start to the day.

Breathe

Relieve tension in the neck and increase lung capacity to diminish stress.

Stand straight with your feet together. Place fingertips under your chin with the fingers clasped and with your elbows touching each other. Inhale slowly for a count of 7 and as you do this bring your elbows up as high as possible. Gently let your head drop back and exhale slowly through your mouth. When you have exhaled bring your head back up slowly as you let your elbows fall to the start position.

Build up to 10 repetitions.

Stretch

Release tension in the lower back and tone your waist and midriff.

Stand straight with your legs at least 3 feet apart, your toes facing forwards. Inhale deeply and lift your right hand in the air. As you exhale, bend to the left side and slide your left hand down your left leg. Go as far as is comfortable. Breathe normally and hold for a count of 7. Increase to 10 as you progress. Inhale and slowly return to an upright position. Exhale and lower your arm.

Repeat to other side and then repeat the whole cycle 3 times.

Bend

Stretch your spine and feel more alert.

Stand straight with your legs together. Inhale and lift your arms up above your head with your palms together. Stretch upwards. Now place your right foot about 3 feet in front of your left foot. Breathe in and lift your arms above your head with palms together once again. As you exhale start to move forwards with your back flat and legs straight. You are aiming for your chin to be around knee level and your hands on the ground. If you can't manage this go as far as you can keeping hands above your head and your back flat. Feel the stretch and remain for a count of 7 breathing normally.

Repeat on other side. You may be able to stretch further on this side.

Now stand straight with your feet apart. Inhale and stretch your arms up in the air. As you exhale, bend forwards with legs straight and back flat and grasp your left leg with your right hand. You are aiming to grasp your foot, but at first go as far as is comfortable. Slowly lift your left arm in the air and turn so you are looking upwards to your left hand. Breathe normally and hold for a count of 7. Then slowly lower your arm and relax forwards clasping both legs with your hands and gently pulling your upper body towards the legs. Breathe normally. As you exhale, grasp your right leg with your left hand and slowly lift your right arm in the air. Turn to look this time at your right hand. Breathe normally for a count of 7.

Again move so that you grasp both legs with both arms and are looking backwards through your legs. Relax into the stretch. Inhale and gradually return to upright position. Now bend backwards, hands at waist with fingers supporting your back exhaling as you reach your maximum stretch point.

Repeat.

Now sit and relax for a couple of minutes with a cup of hot water and lemon. A perfect start to the day.

An everyday miracle

Sometimes we all hope for miracles to get us through tough times. Ever considered conjuring your own?

Ask a question, end up with a miracle. Sounds dodgy, but it's about finding what works and doing it often. Far easier than changing what you – or your friends and family – do wrong.

It's part of a kind of therapy called brief solution-focused therapy. Here is the miracle question:

'Suppose one night there is a miracle while you are asleep and your problem is solved. What do you suppose you will notice different the next morning that will tell you there has been a miracle?'

Grab a pen and paper, re-read the miracle question, and jot down imagined changes in as much detail as you can muster. Try and include small, tell-tale signs that would let you know there is something different. Who would be the first person to notice something different about you after the miracle? What would your partner/children/parents/friends/Pilates instructor notice was different about you if there had been a miracle? What would they all do differently? What would be different in your relationship with them?

Suspend reality and pretend your miracle has happened. And ask yourself these toughies: What will you need to do differently at work? What will you need to do differently at home? What will be the first thing your grumpy boss/bitchy colleagues/whining children will notice about you and the way you behave if the miracle had happened? What will they do differently?

If you've been jotting answers down, you might have had a Eureka moment. If you haven't, don't worry.

The catch? You're the one who does the altering. But you're already well on your way. Answering these questions helps you find ways out. So next time you think 'only a miracle could get me out of this mess', remember: there can be a miracle, because you can produce one.

Pretend your miracle has happened

Solution workshop

Are you looking for ways of coping with problems? Try these tried and trusted problem-solving strategies.

Problems with partners, friends, health, work or money are one of our biggest drains. So it's hardly surprising that researchers at Oxford University found that problem-solving reduces depression, anxiety and hopelessness.

Follow this seven-step formula for problem-solving:

1. Start by writing down problems that are bothering you.

2. Overwhelmed with problems? Pick one at a time. Choose the problem that worries you most or, conversely, pick one that is easier to solve.

3. Go from the general to the specific. Once you've picked your problem, try to rewrite it in a specific way. That means you'll know when your problem is solved. For instance, not 'I'm so poor' but 'I can't afford to pay the gas bill'. When you're not worried by the gas bill because it's paid or you've negotiated with the company, you'll know you've made progress.

4. Identify different options by brainstorming. Get a big bit of paper. Scribble down as many possible solutions as you can. These questions should help:

- *What's worked before?*
- *If my best friend had this problem, what would I suggest?*
- *What would mum, dad or someone else I trust advise?*

Include everything, as even zany or outlandish stuff can help you think quickly and creatively.

5. Examine every solution, weighing up pros and cons. When you've got a list of options, think through the pros and cons of each. You might like to draw up a table with the pros and cons.

6. Pick the solution that has the most pros. As you think of the pros and cons, run each option through this two-question filter:

- *Will it help?*
- *Can I do it?*

7. Plan steps you'll take to put your chosen solution into action and go for it.

Imagine...

Yearning for a calming, captivating technique to soothe your soul? Find out how visualisation can relax and revive you.

Visualisation means using your mind to create pictures. Use it to relax, fall asleep or feel better fast.

Creating pictures or scenes in your mind's eye is a great way to relax, but can be used in other ways as well. Visualisation helped women suffering from postnatal depression. Researchers observed women who had just had their first baby for the first four weeks following the births. Women who took part in visualisation techniques had reduced depression and anxiety but also improved self-esteem compared to women who didn't.

If you want to have a go, the best way to start is using visualisation techniques to relax.

Find a quiet place where you won't be disturbed. For a few minutes close your eyes. Cast your mind back to the time in your life you felt most deeply relaxed. Some people like to think of a holiday, but feel free to choose anywhere. Imagine yourself in that calm place now. Try to bring it to life vividly, using all your senses. What can you see? What can you hear? What can you taste? What can you smell? What can you feel? Stay in that place as long as it takes to feel calm. It needs practice, but once you can picture your calming place, you can escape there whenever you want. And every time you go, it gets easier.

Creating pictures in your mind's eye can help you achieve things you never thought possible. Nobody's really sure how this works, but one idea is that visualisation stimulates the right half of your brain – that's the part dealing with emotions and creativity. In most people, the left half is responsible for reasoning, verbal ability and making logical conclusions. Stimulating the right half balances out the left, leaving you more relaxed and able to see things in a quirkier way.

No success at job interviews? Visualisation helps you make a great first impression and maximise your performance. Fears about rejection can make you overcautious, under-confident and look defeated before you've even started. Imagine your wildest dreams coming true. Visualise wowing the panel with your answers, excelling at presentations, speaking fluently and articulately, and then being offered the job. Enjoy it. How does it feel? Of course, no one can promise it will go like that on the day, but mental dress rehearsals will help you give your best performance. Cultivating optimism and enthusiasm will positively affect interviewers' response to you and, if you're not offered the job this time, it'll help you bounce back rather than sinking into desolation.

Visualisation can help fine-tune your intuition. Instead of predicting how things are going to end up, why not make a list of all the possible solutions to your deep-rooted problems and imagine each solution is written on a door. Now imagine yourself going through each door in turn. What do you find on the other side? If it's not what you'd like, cross back over the threshold and go through a different door.

If this is difficult, buy a notebook and begin writing down your imagined fantasy life. Want to lose weight? Don't meander on about how badly your latest diet is going. Instead fill four pages along the lines of 'I am looking the best I've ever looked, wearing fabulous, fashionable clothes.' Go into detail. Bored at work? 'I am working at a fulfilling job which uses all my abilities and strengths. I am admired by my colleagues and feel I contribute good work. My boss loves me and I am given a great bonus.' Writing it down makes your fantasy more real. You feel better as you write. The fantasy begins to feel true. Before you know it, aspects of it begin to come true.

Make a list of all the possible solutions to your deep-rooted problems

Oprah Winfrey's secrets to serenity

She has devoted her life to being the best that she can be, and helping others do the same. And she's got very rich doing it. What has she learned?

'Life is a journey. Everyday experiences will teach you who you really are.'

'When people show you who they are, believe them the first time. This is especially helpful with men. Don't force them to beat you over the head with the message.'

'Turn your wounds into wisdom. Everyone makes mistakes. They are just God's way of telling you you're moving in the wrong direction.'

'Be grateful. Keep a daily journal of the things you are thankful for. It will keep you focused on the abundance in your life.'

'Create the highest, grandest vision possible for your life because you become what you believe.'

Four

Detox your life

Up until now you may have been feeling too fed up to make concrete physical changes. But with some of the feel-good techniques outlined in the last three sections in place, you should be ready to turbo-drive your attempts to feel better. Nothing works quite as well as ridding yourself of the unwanted and unnecessary.

Quiz:
How cluttered is your world?

Surrounded by chaos? Surplus stuff? Have a lengthy to-do list of chores to do around the home/garden/office that's taking on a life of its own? It's easy to get overwhelmed by clutter, but it can take over – and if your living or working space is not your sanctuary then you're not in control. Remember, if you feel in control, you are in control.

So before you embark on that major tidy up campaign, let's assess the kind of clutterer you are. Perhaps your home is an oasis of calm, but your office is a maelstrom of files, discarded newspapers, unopened post. For some, the wardrobe/bedroom is the war zone – too many outfits, too many 'fat' or 'thin' options, too many choices, too little time to wear them all.

Or it could be it's your diary that's out of control – just too many outings, school paraphernalia, daily must-dos and endless appointments that mean you rarely know what on earth's going on from one day to the next.

For some of us it's sheer lack of space, for others it's storage, for others it's peace of mind.

The following questionnaires should help you assess your weak spots, and identify how to go forward in the journey of decluttering.

How disorganised are you really?

Part one: Tick the statements below which apply to you

1. I have more clothes/books/magazines/saucepans than cupboard space. ☐
2. I can never find those vital things I need when I'm whizzing out the door – keys, sunglasses, purse. ☐
3. I'm a fashion addict – can't get enough clothes and shoes. ☐
4. I'm not sure what colour carpet I have in the bedroom. ☐

5. I bought my home because I had a vision for the garden – but it's a wilderness out there. ☐
6. I can't throw anything away – you never know when you might need those receipts. ☐
7. I can organise myself but you try organising a partner, three children and a dog. ☐
8. I often miss appointments and turn up late for events. ☐
9. I love souvenirs – I get really attached to certain possessions. ☐
10. I'm a creative person; er, they say creativity thrives in chaos don't they? ☐

How did you score?

- If you ticked one or two statements it means you could do with being a bit more organised, but your life is probably not adversely affected by clutter.

- Three to five ticks means you're in danger of becoming inefficient, tired and stressed.

- If you ticked five or more statements it's a miracle you get anything done – let alone this quiz. It's time to take yourself in hand and get some order into your life.

Part two: Tick which statements best apply to you

1. How would you describe your home:

(a) Chaos everywhere – it's a sea of books, CDs, papers, shoes and random items in no fixed abode. ☐

(b) Most rooms are immaculate – but I have small pockets of mess – things I rarely use, but somehow can't stand to throw away. ☐

(c) I try to tidy up once a week but I'm so busy the clutter tends to build up. ☐

(d) I'm fairly clean and tidy, but never have enough space for my stuff. ☐

2. Which statement best describes your attitude to time-keeping and sticking to a schedule

(a) I have a diary somewhere – if I could just lay my hands on it. ☐

(b) I tend to say yes to everything – don't want to miss out on anything. But I'm often late or have to cancel at the last minute. ☐

(c) Most of the time I'm in control – but in very busy periods it goes belly up. ☐

(d) I'm not a 'diary' person; I tend to keep events/must dos in my head – I've got a good memory. ☐

3. How would you best describe your working style?
(a) My office is rather cluttered – I sort of know where everything is – but I'm a creative, disordered person – that's my charm. ☐
(b) I have back-up files for my back-up files – I daren't throw anything away in case it's the very paper or file I need. ☐
(c) I don't have the luxury of being able to tidy up; there's no time to organise myself as my working day is fast and furious. ☐
(d) I muddle through, but I have such a heavy workload and a tiny office/work space I just don't have the time to keep it pristine. ☐

How did you score?

Mostly As: It sounds as though you're naturally a bit of a clutterbug. You could really benefit from a **system**; start by deciding where important items are going to be kept – and resolve to put them back.

Mostly Bs: You're too **sentimental** about stuff – and perhaps a bit insecure so you're holding on to things *just in case*… It's time to get tough – keep a few choice things for old times' sake, and get rid of the rest.

Mostly Cs: Chances are you're **time-pressured**, rather than innately messy. Could you afford someone to help around the house? Consider setting aside one day a month for some serious organisation, so that even if clutter accumulates during busy periods, it will only take one or two sessions to get back on track.

Mostly Ds: You're pretty organised, but you lack the **equipment** to get on top of things – start with investing in some better storage, try to create more space at home. Treat yourself to a diary, and a rub-clean notice board, and a jotter or notepad to keep abreast of things.

Streamline your systems

We're talking about the avalanche of paper, magazines, unpaid bills, flyers for pizza houses, the general detritus of twenty-first century life that threatens to overwhelm you.

Not to mention your kitchen surfaces. Try this system and you will finally live in a clear home. Its only disadvantage is that it takes some time to set up. But even if your paperwork is in turmoil, if you have a day to spend or ten free hours, give it a go. Ten hours can work magic and then you're set up for life.

Step 1. Gather together everything that you need to create order in your world. Cardboard magazine holders, folders, pens, labels, stapler, a couple of hard backed address books (personal and business), not forgetting a huge industrial-strength bin-bag. Also keep the family calendar and diary at hand so you can put dates directly into them as you uncover them.

Step 2. Work systematically. You are going to go from one side of your desk to the other, or one side of the room to the other. Gather together one pile of paper and assorted junk and place it bang in the middle of the room or your desk. Start sorting. Every single piece of paper that you touch must be actioned.

- If it contains a phone number that you might need in the future, then put the number straight into one of your address books.

- If it is a bill that has to be paid, or anything which must be acted on immediately, then create a file for urgent and unpaid bills.

- If it is an article or piece of information that you might need in the future but which is not urgent, start creating files for these (named files) such as 'pensions', 'holidays', 'general interest'.

Ten hours can work magic

- If it is a piece of information that you need to act on or read or make a decision on but not now, put it in a file marked 'To Do' and make an appointment in your diary sometime in the next week when you'll deal with it. This file should be somewhere accessible and you should clear it not less than once every two weeks or it gets out of control.

- Keep a tickle book. Tickle as in 'tickle my memory'. An A4 hard notebook works well. In it note down the names of anything you might need in the future: the idea for a piece of work, or the name of a savings account offering great interest with the number (so you can throw out the flyer). With a tickle book you don't have to hold on to endless bits of paper just in case you need the information. Keep it by your side at work and if anyone calls with something you might be interested in, scribble it down. Same with emails – with the tickle book you can take down a few words and immediately delete the email so you don't have to litter up your inbox.

Feel good now: *Leave holes in your diary on every day of the week. Don't fill these holes up with stuff. Use them to relax.*

Virtual decluttering

The pre-contemplation phase can help those who find this hard. In whatever room of your home you are in right now, start looking around and dividing the items mentally into one of the following categories – virtually sorting it. Beginning to see every item you touch can get you to the place where you can let things go very fast indeed. It also helps when you're shopping and stops you coming home with stuff that you're not even very sure of in the shop that you want.

I love this item and really need it
Keep it

I don't love it and really don't need this item any more
Throw it

I'm not sure how I feel about this item and I'm not sure that I really need it
Add to maybe pile

I definitely don't love this item but I do need this item
Upgrade with a new replacement that you love

Clean and serene

Don't despair, reach for the duster of dharma and clean your way to a calm, steady disposition.

Cleaning is not a destination, it is a journey. Many a woman (and man) has lost herself in the idea that you have to keep things pristine all the time in order for them to be clean. If you do that, you'll be exhausted all the time.

No, you have to turn to Hindu religious texts to sort this one out. On the eve of an impossible battle, Lord Krishna spoke to Arjuna the warrior king and explained the concept of dharma or caste duty. Dharma means that if you're a warrior, the winning or losing isn't your problem, it's the fighting that matters. You are duty-bound to fight.

In modern terms this means that the end result of your actions is not what is important, it's conscientiously carrying them out. I know, I know, it's a bit of a stretch to ask you to imagine that Lord Krishna was referring to bed-making when he talked of dharma but there is a case for saying, don't fret too much that they'll have to be remade tomorrow and the day after tomorrow and the day after that ad nauseam. Just get on with it in a spirit of being in the moment.

Cleaning can be really therapeutic. You can lose yourself in the grain of wood as you're polishing it. See rainbow worlds in bubbles when you're doing the washing up. You'd be hard pushed to see much in a dirty oven but hey, it's great exercise to be scrubbing away on your knees.

The other important thing to remember is that your family and you are in it together, so don't feel like you have to do everything. No one will do you for child labour if you get the kids to occasionally undertake a little light dusting and even toddlers can be taught to put their toys away in a toy box when they're done playing. Teach your kids from a very early age to be responsible for their own toys (though beware that other people's children and their capacity to wreak havoc may leave you reeling in horror).

Still, even if you can't get your little ones in on the act, your life partner can definitely do his or her bit. Split your chores according to personal preferences or attribute each chore a number 1–6 and throw a dice to decide who does what. Introduce an element of fun into your cleaning and you'll soon be relaxing with a glass of wine, surveying your clean and serene domain.

If you really hate cleaning think seriously about whether you can afford to hire someone to do it for you. If you can, then do that. Alternatively, look at bartering your services. Perhaps you're brilliant at making cakes or DIY? Swap with family and friends so that they do your cleaning and you do the things they don't want to do. If you really can't bear cleaning, try also to keep your possessions to a minimum as then you won't have as much to clean.

No one will do you for child labour if you occasionally get the kids to undertake a little light dusting

Clean up your finances

Messy finances have a way of wreaking havoc over other areas of your life.

Picture the scene. You've been flexing that new credit card far too much. So perhaps you fall behind on your payments. Perhaps you get into a bad habit of spending more than you earned – for the fifth month running. You feel yourself sliding into debt. Your overdraft limit is looming, and you're only half way through the month. You would try to pay the phone bill but you can't remember where you left it – probably in the same pile as all those receipts/papers for your tax bill form. Oh dear.

Your partner gets wind of the credit card gymnastics and isn't happy. The stress starts to take its toll on your health. You borrow more to get back on track, but end up further in debt with crippling interest rates. Bailiffs come a-knocking. Partner leaves you for younger, more solvent model. House repossessed. Life in tatters. Die alone surrounded by cats.

See what happens when you don't take your finances by the proverbials?

OK, the above is unlikely. But the fact that you've kept reading this far shows that somewhere in you lurks guilt about how you manage your money. That's so draining, so let's give it up.

Start by assessing just how organised you are when it comes to income, outgoings – and striking that fine balance. Are you sensibly thinking of the future? Is your pension plan a winner? Do you actually have a pension? Do you invest wisely? Do you actually have a savings plan?

When it comes to getting your finances in check, you need to clarify your objectives: Tick any of the following that apply to you. It may also be worth cutting the list out, or copying it on to a big piece of paper and sticking it on the wall to remind you why you've finally resolved to get more money-organised.

1. I want to get out of debt. ☐
2. I'd like to be able to lay my hands on important bills/receipts/statements without having to turn the house or office upside down. ☐
3. I'd like to start saving. ☐
4. I'd like to be mortgage-free within the next ten years. ☐
5. I'd like to be more punctual and organised when it comes to paying bills – no more red ones! ☐
6. I need to feel calmer and less flustered when it comes to my finances. ☐
7. I need to start planning for my children's future – university fees etc. ☐

8. I'd like to overhaul the way I spend my money. ☐
9. I'd like to be able to make more money without doing more work! ☐
10. I'd like to get savvy about the stock market. ☐
11. I'd like to know how to get everything cheaper – give me some bargain-hunter basics. ☐
12. I'd just like to start afresh... ☐

If you ticked four or more, you need a financial makeover – pronto. Read on.

Getting organised:

It doesn't take long for finances to spiral out of control. Paying bills on time, keeping track of those receipts so you can meet your tax return deadline, and keeping abreast of your weekly budget is easier if your financial paperwork is organised. By sorting and filing fastidiously, you'll be less likely to let your credit card mount up, or forget to cancel direct debits. Plus you will be less likely to have an unbridled spending spree if you know what's in your account.

In this section we'll explore some great ideas for getting more money-savvy and taking control of your expenditure.

Try these tips for starters:

- Why not keep a spending diary for a month? Write down every penny you spend – *everything* – from that newspaper, those new shoes, daily cappuccinos, to the bills, mortgage, childcare, meals out. That way you know exactly how much you're spending – and what you can really afford.

- Reduce your financial clutter. Buy several files and label them – bills, invoices, pay slips, and receipts separated into boxes for 'clothes,' 'household stuff', 'car' and so on. It's a really effective way to help you keep track of your spending, useful in case you need to change things/take purchases back.

- Keep all your receipts or post in one place, go through them every week or so, then file them regularly.

- Sit down and pay all bills in one go, write 'paid' on each, file them. Assess which bills would be easier to keep track of, plus cheaper, if you paid them by direct debit.

- Check your bank statement once or twice a month to keep track of funds. Switching to an online account means you can check it when you like and may help get rid of some of that annoying paperwork.

- Invest in a shredder for old bank statements/credit card bills so you can bin excess paperwork without worrying who may find your personal details. Recycle the old paper waste. Or start banking and paying bills etc. online – much easier, less clutter.

It doesn't take long for finances to spiral out of control

The time of your life

If you're feeling weighed down by tasks, you'll find that good time management is an irresistible way to transform your mood and your life.

Whether you want to take a break from the rat race or just want to find the energy to keep up, read on.

Think strategically

Feeling inundated with all those things you need to do? Using to-do lists decreases stress, develops great organisational skills and improves your memory. Just writing things down means you are 25% more likely to do them. However, don't be a slave to a daily 'to-do' list. See the big picture. On Monday morning lose the sinking 'I've got so much to do' sensation. Instead, think 'what are my goals for this week?' Decide what you want to have done by Friday and then break each goal into smaller tasks that have to be undertaken to achieve all you want by Friday. Slot these tasks in throughout your week. This helps you prioritise so that the tricky and difficult things, or tasks that depend on other people's input, don't sink to the back of your consciousness. It also means you are giving attention to all that you have to do and not spending too much time on one task at the beginning of the week. Concentrate on three or four items on your 'to-do' list at once. You won't be so overwhelmed.

Work with your energy levels

Lots of us are sluggish in the mornings, but you can sneak up to fifteen minutes extra in bed by a bit of planning the night before. Put cereal (minus milk) into a bowl, fill the kettle and put out a mug. Take out the next day's clothes. There's nothing worse than getting up and needing to iron a shirt.

Look at your day and work out when you have the most energy. Block out that time to be creative and don't allow those times to be impinged upon by meetings and phone calls that could be done any time.

Communication, communication, communication

Make the phone call you're dreading. Right now. That call saps your energy all day so just do it.

Have meetings in the morning. Other people are fresh. Meetings held in the afternoon when everyone is sluggish drag on.

Check emails three times a day and limit how long you spend replying. Morning, lunch and before you leave. That's it. Keeping to this means your working day isn't frittered away in pointless emailing.

Limit phone calls in the same way. Make a list of calls you have to make that day. Call first thing. If someone isn't there, leave a message and ask them to call you back at your next 'phone period'. Just before lunch is good. That means neither of you will linger over the call. Your other 'phone time' could be around 4.30 p.m. for the same reason. Of course you can't limit phone calls completely to these times but most of us can control our incoming calls better than we do. By putting calls in the context of a busy working day, you keep them shorter. Social chat is important and nice but most of us spend too much time on it. This goes for personal chats too. Give a friend five minutes, no longer. Or better still, save the chat as a reward for a hard-working morning.

Break it down

When you're overwhelmed by a job, break it into a series of smaller, simpler tasks. For instance, instead of feeling overwhelmed because your house is in a mess, set yourself a daily fifteen-minute spurt, and work through it room by room. Too low and weary to fill in another job application form? Start with the easy questions you don't need to think about, like your name, address and date of birth. Once you've got some momentum going, add in things that need more concentration, like your job history. And start big tasks as soon as you can. Spending 10 minutes a day for a fortnight will get a difficult task done effortlessly; spending the same time the day before your deadline will be stressful and annoying and you'll probably end up spending far longer on the task than you need to.

Break each goal into smaller tasks that have to be undertaken to achieve all you want

Clear your space, clear your head

1. *One in, one out. Make it a rule: for every new item that comes into your life, you need to get rid of one. This will dramatically reduce the amount of money you spend. Think about it. Every time you buy a new CD or book or pair of shoes, you have to get rid of one.*

2. *If it's flat, keep it clear. A room looks so much cleaner if all flat surfaces, from the floor to tabletops to countertops, are clear of clutter. Remove everything from these surfaces except what makes your space beautiful.*

3. *Designate a home for everything. If stuff doesn't have a home in your home, you need to get rid of it.*

4. *Declutter every month. Make the last weekend of every month the one where you declutter. Or be less rigid. Experiment to see what interval works for your life. Try a couple of one-hour sessions per week.*

Try the 40–20 rule: 40 minute graft followed by 20 minutes self-congratulatory gloating. You get better at decluttering, soon it's second nature. Find a home for everything you own that is useful or beautiful. You're allowed one drawer as a glory hole for all those odd things you can't think where to put.

5. *Enjoy what you have. Are you always buying stuff? If so, is it out of real necessity, or do you just like to buy stuff? It's important that you take a look at these desires, and see if you can address them. Reducing your desires will go a long way to reducing your need to fight clutter.*

6. *Change the way you live. Clutter didn't create itself. How did it get there? Do you buy a lot? Do you refuse to put things away?*

Managing your relationships

Hell is other people. Time to detox your address book.

All around you are the energy black holes people who are unhappy, negative or angry and would like nothing more than to drag you into their stressful world. And there is absolutely nothing you can do about them. The only thing you can change is your attitude. (There is a proviso to this – if your life is littered with difficult people out to get you, then it could be something to do with your expectations.) But sometimes, even most times, it's not you – it's them.

Other people have their own agenda. You can't know what they are and you can't change them. Take a tip from yoga teacher and author, Rosamond Richardson. She recommends visualising yourself surrounded by white light, creating a protective bubble around you. Negativity just bounces off this white light and can't affect you. Spend a couple of minutes doing this on your way to work and see how effective it is the more that you practise it.

Another way of distancing yourself from other people's dramas is to realise that a lot of stress in our relationships with other people comes from trying to second guess what they're thinking or what their intention is. Try saying: 'What other people think of me is none of my business'. Think about that statement closely. It sounds counterintuitive but it's profoundly true. You have little or no control over what

'What other people think of me is none of my business'

they choose to think, only in your own response. When you start believing that what they think has nothing to do with you, life gets a whole lot easier.

Another useful way of turning relationships around is to think of ways you can rephrase problems so that rather than expressing what's wrong, you express what you want from the relationship. For instance say 'I want to have my ideas respected' rather than 'My boss is such a wet blanket'. Or 'I want to be equally responsible in our relationship' rather than 'My husband always decides where we eat'. It gives you a framework of how to behave in order to get what you want. The sentences that begin 'I' give you options; in the others, you're a victim of another's behaviour which ultimately, you can't do anything to change.

These tips work in any circumstance, but there is no point in denying they are a lot harder to put into practice when the people who upset you are those you share a home, a bed, a life with. Again, don't waste time dwelling on how less stressful life would be if John was only kinder, mum was less depressing, and Emily less of a cow. You can do nothing to control that except take control of yourself and your own reactions.

Try this exercise: make a list of the people with whom you have regular contact. Then divide the list into three categories.

- The energisers. They look after you in every way. They give great advice. They are interested in you and care what happens to you. They bring happiness to your life.

- The neutral. They're OK. Fine to spend a few hours with adding little, taking little. They may be sweet people but in the end they don't enrich your life.

- The drainers. They are people who don't deliver, let you down, bring you down. They're users, gossips, people whose conversation brings you down – even if you find it entertaining, it makes you feel bad about yourself afterwards.

It is fairly obvious what you should do from here. But the value of this exercise is in realising what sort of energiser:drainer ratio you have operating in your life. Often we don't realise just how much of our misery is caused by people around us, people who have taken up residence in our lives for years without us realising their toxic effect. Limit time with the drainers, and if they happen to be your closest friends, your family, your lover, you need to think about that very closely. You may feel unable to cut them out now (although that is an option) but you can limit the time they are allowed to suck you into their world.

Just say 'no'

If you're a people pleaser, you'll know that if you always say yes to others, you're taken for granted.

Now and then, all of us have to do things that don't benefit us much in order to feel that we're pulling our weight. But if it's a daily occurrence then we're going to get run down and ill. Worse, we're going to get seriously fed up.

Answer true or false to each of these statements.

- I can't relax until I finish all the things I have to do. T/F
- If I wasn't doing favours for other people most days I wouldn't think much of myself. T/F
- I seldom say no to a work colleague or family member who asks a favour of me. T/F
- I often find myself changing my own plans or working day to fit in with other people's wants. T/F
- I rarely, if ever, feel comfortable with what I've accomplished. T/F
- I often feel I'm so exhausted that I don't have time for my own interests. T/F
- I feel guilty relaxing. T/F
- I find myself saying 'yes' to others when inside a voice is saying 'no, no, no'. T/F
- I honestly believe that if I stop doing things for others they'd think less of me. T/F
- I find it hard to ask other people to do things for me. T/F

How did you score?

Add up the number of Ts you circled. If your score is between 7 and 10, you think it more important to please others than to please yourself. If it's between 4 and 6, you should be careful. You're on the slippery slope to terminal niceness. If you score 3 or less, you're good at saying no and keep your own needs in balance with those of others.

For all of you who scored more than 3:

- Try an intermediate stage. Next time someone asks you to do something you don't want to do, say 'I'm not sure. Let me get back to you'. The breather is often enough to stiffen your resolve.

- Think of situations where you need to say no more. Imagine yourself in these situations saying no. Practise the exercise in front of a mirror if necessary. It makes it much easier in real-life situations.

- Whenever you're asked to do something ask yourself 'do I really want to do this?' rather than ask yourself 'should I do this?' If you don't want to do it, let other people pick up the baton.

- When you say no, keep it short. 'Sorry. No', is best of all. Very rarely will there be any call for you to feel defensive or make apologies. However, if that's too hardcore, here are some nice ways of saying no:

  Let's go for a swim.
  Sorry, I really don't enjoy swimming.

  Fancy coming back for a coffee?
  No, I can't stay out late as I've got an early start tomorrow.

  Let's meet at the gym after work.
  I'd really rather not go to the gym today.

  Why don't you come to the sales with me?
  Maybe you'd better ask someone else; I'm not mad for shopping.

- Try using body language to back up what you say. Shaking your head, while saying no, is a good start.

Katharine Hepburn's secrets to happiness

The great actor had a difficult personal life and saw many ups and downs in her career. How did she cope?

'Accept life. You plough ahead and make a hit. And you plough on and someone passes you. Then someone passes them. Time levels.'

'I don't think that work ever really destroyed anybody. I think that lack of work destroys them a hell of a lot more.'

'I never lose sight of the fact that just being is fun.'

Index